AF599209

River Adventures
THE MISSISSIPPI RIVER
BY COLLEEN SEXTON
BLASTOFF! DISCOVERY
BELLWETHER MEDIA • MINNEAPOLIS, MN

This edition first published in 2025 by Bellwether Media, Inc.

Library of Congress Cataloging-in-Publication Data

Names: Sexton, Colleen, author.
Title: The Mississippi River / by Colleen Sexton.
Description: Minneapolis, MN : Bellwether Media, Inc., 2025. | Series: Blastoff! Discovery: River Adventures | Includes bibliographical references and index. | Audience: Ages 7-13 | Audience: Grades 4-6 | Summary: "Engaging images accompany information about the Mississippi River. The combination of high-interest subject matter and narrative text is intended for students in grades 3 through 8"– Provided by publisher.
Identifiers: LCCN 2024016552 (print) | LCCN 2024016553 (ebook) | ISBN 9798886879995 (library binding) | ISBN 9781644879313 (ebook)
Subjects: LCSH: Mississippi River–Juvenile literature.
Classification: LCC F351 .S388 2025 (print) | LCC F351 (ebook) | DDC 977–dc23/eng/20240411
LC record available at https://lccn.loc.gov/2024016552
LC ebook record available at https://lccn.loc.gov/2024016553

Editor: Rachael Barnes Designer: Brittany McIntosh

Printed in the United States of America, North Mankato, MN.

TABLE OF CONTENTS

ON THE MISSISSIPPI RIVER

LAKE WINNIBIGOSHISH

Dawn breaks on a chilly morning in northern Minnesota. Two campers load gear into a canoe. They push off and paddle downstream on the Mississippi River. As they round a bend, geese honk overhead. The campers spot a deer through tall grasses that line the waterway.

A GREAT NAME

The Mississippi River gets its name from the Ojibwe word *misi-ziibi*. It means "great river" or "gathering of waters."

The river widens, and the canoe enters Lake Winnibigoshish. The campers stay close to shore. They rejoin the river where it flows out of the lake. At midday, the campers rest on the shoreline and watch the fast-moving water. What a beautiful day on the Mississippi River!

GEOGRAPHY

WHERE THE RIVER BEGINS

The Mississippi begins as a small stream. It is only 18 feet (5.5 meters) wide and about 18 inches (46 centimeters) deep. Itasca State Park's visitors can hop across the river on a stone path!

ITASCA STATE PARK

The Mississippi River is about 2,340 miles (3,766 kilometers) long. It trickles out of Lake Itasca in northern Minnesota. The river flows northeastward and then turns south. It runs along the borders of nine other states before it empties into the **Gulf** of Mexico.

The Mississippi River connects much of the United States and passes through several major cities. It runs between Minneapolis and St. Paul in Minnesota. Farther south, it reaches St. Louis, Missouri, and Memphis, Tennessee. Finally, it flows past Baton Rouge and New Orleans in Louisiana.

BIG AND BIGGER!

The Mississippi River is the second-longest river in North America. At around 2,540 miles (4,088 kilometers) long, the Missouri River is the longest!

CONFLUENCE OF THE MISSOURI AND MISSISSIPPI RIVERS

The Mississippi River formed over millions of years. Thick **glaciers** moved across northern parts of North America. They carved a broad valley. About 12,000 years ago, the glaciers melted. Water rushed south, creating a path for the Mississippi and about 250 **tributaries**.

OHIO RIVER

The Illinois and Missouri Rivers are major tributaries in the Mississippi River Valley. They join the Mississippi River near St. Louis. Downstream, the Mississippi River's volume more than doubles at its **confluence** with the Ohio River. The Arkansas and Red Rivers join farther south.

The Mississippi River is widest at Lake Winnibigoshish in Minnesota. It reaches over 11 miles (18 kilometers) wide. Downstream, the river curves between tall, rocky cliffs. In places, the water flows quickly. South of St. Louis, the Mississippi slows as the land flattens. The river then winds across a wide valley.

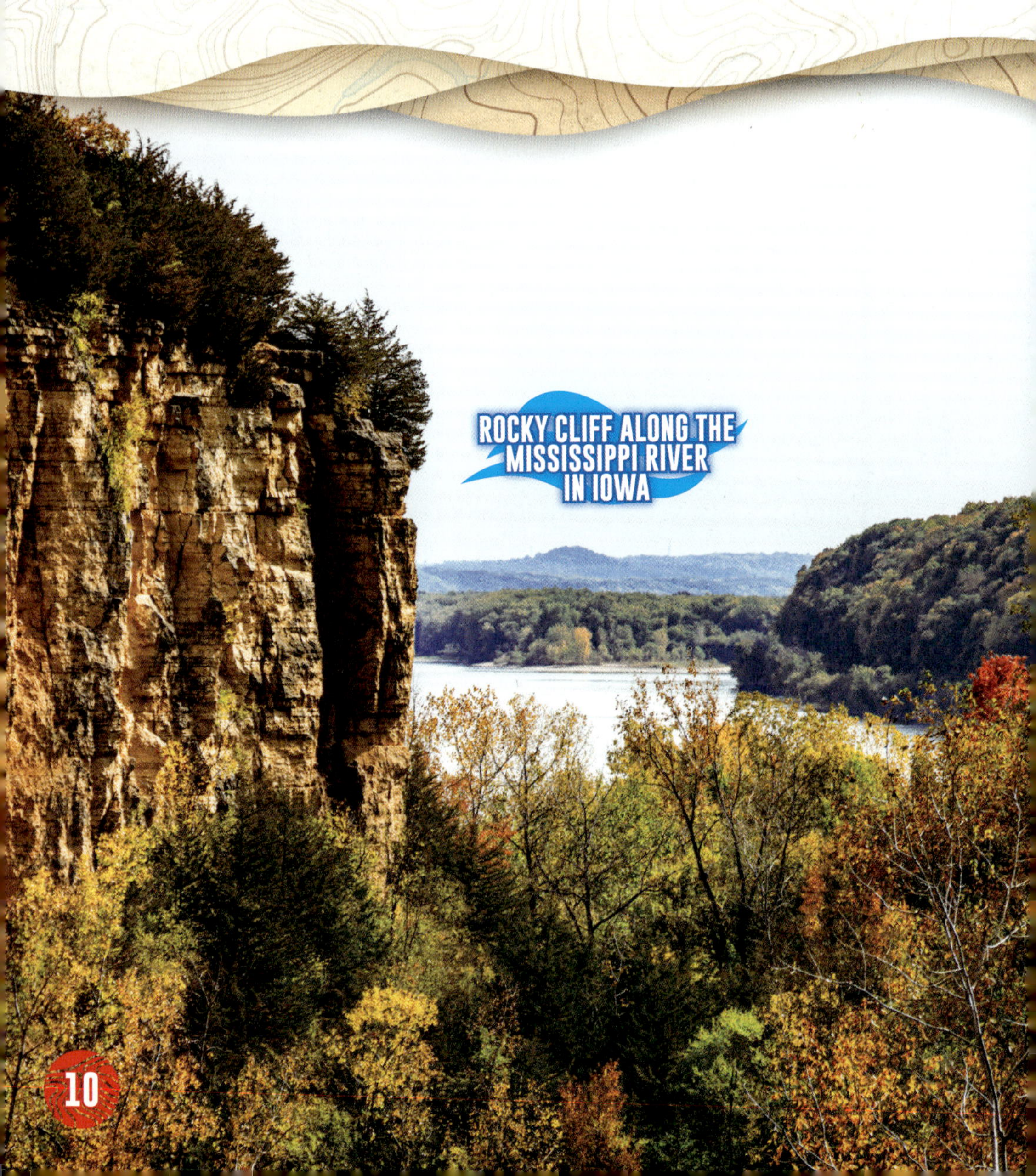

ROCKY CLIFF ALONG THE MISSISSIPPI RIVER IN IOWA

RIVER ISLANDS

More than 750 islands dot the waters of the Mississippi River.

MISSISSIPPI RIVER DELTA

The river's deepest point lies near Algiers Point in New Orleans. It is about 200 feet (61 meters) deep! Farther south, the waterway breaks into several **channels**. They flow through the river's **delta** into the Gulf of Mexico.

PLANTS AND ANIMALS

Many plants and animals live along the Mississippi River. In the north, thick forests of birch, oak, and maple trees line the riverbanks. Squirrels and chipmunks run along the trees' branches. Deer nibble on leaves. Coyotes and bobcats compete for prey. At night, frogs croak as foxes and skunks chase mice.

Bass, sunfish, and trout swim in the river's current. Muskrats, otters, and beavers build homes near shore. Rattlesnakes wind through tall grasses on cliffs. Eagles and owls fly overhead. Ducks and geese fly south along the river.

EASTERN GRAY SQUIRREL

GREEN FROG

LARGEMOUTH BASS

BOBCAT

MALLARD DUCKS

NORTH AMERICAN BEAVER

Life Span: 10 to 12 years
Status: least concern

North American beaver range =

As the Mississippi flows south, cottonwood, pecan, and willow trees grow along the river. Cattails poke above shallow waters where catfish and carp swim. Mussels burrow into the muddy river bottom. Louisiana black bears roam the area.

FOLLOW THE RIVER

Every year about 325 species of birds follow the Mississippi River. The river is part of the Mississippi Flyway. This route stretches from the Arctic Circle into Central and South America.

AMERICAN WHITE PELICAN

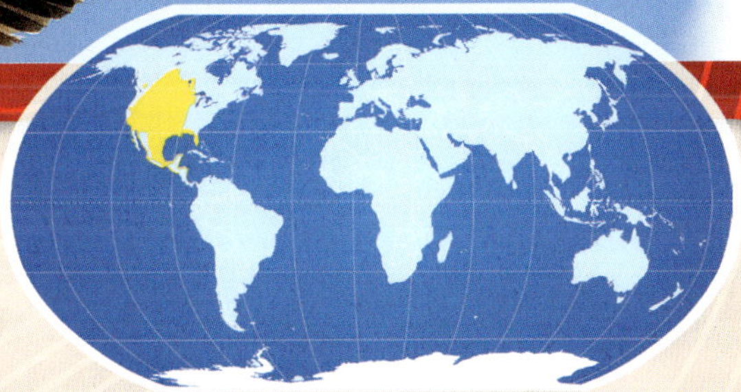

Life Span: up to 26 years

Status: least concern

American white pelican range =

LEAST CONCERN	NEAR THREATENED	VULNERABLE	ENDANGERED	CRITICALLY ENDANGERED	EXTINCT IN THE WILD	EXTINCT
▲						

Water that enters the delta creates a swamp. Spanish moss and orchids wrap around the branches of bald cypress and tupelo trees. Snapping turtles feed on fish and river plants. Pelicans, herons, and other birds walk in shallow waters. They pluck out shrimp, oysters, and crayfish to eat. Nearby, alligators slide through the water in search of prey.

HUMAN HISTORY

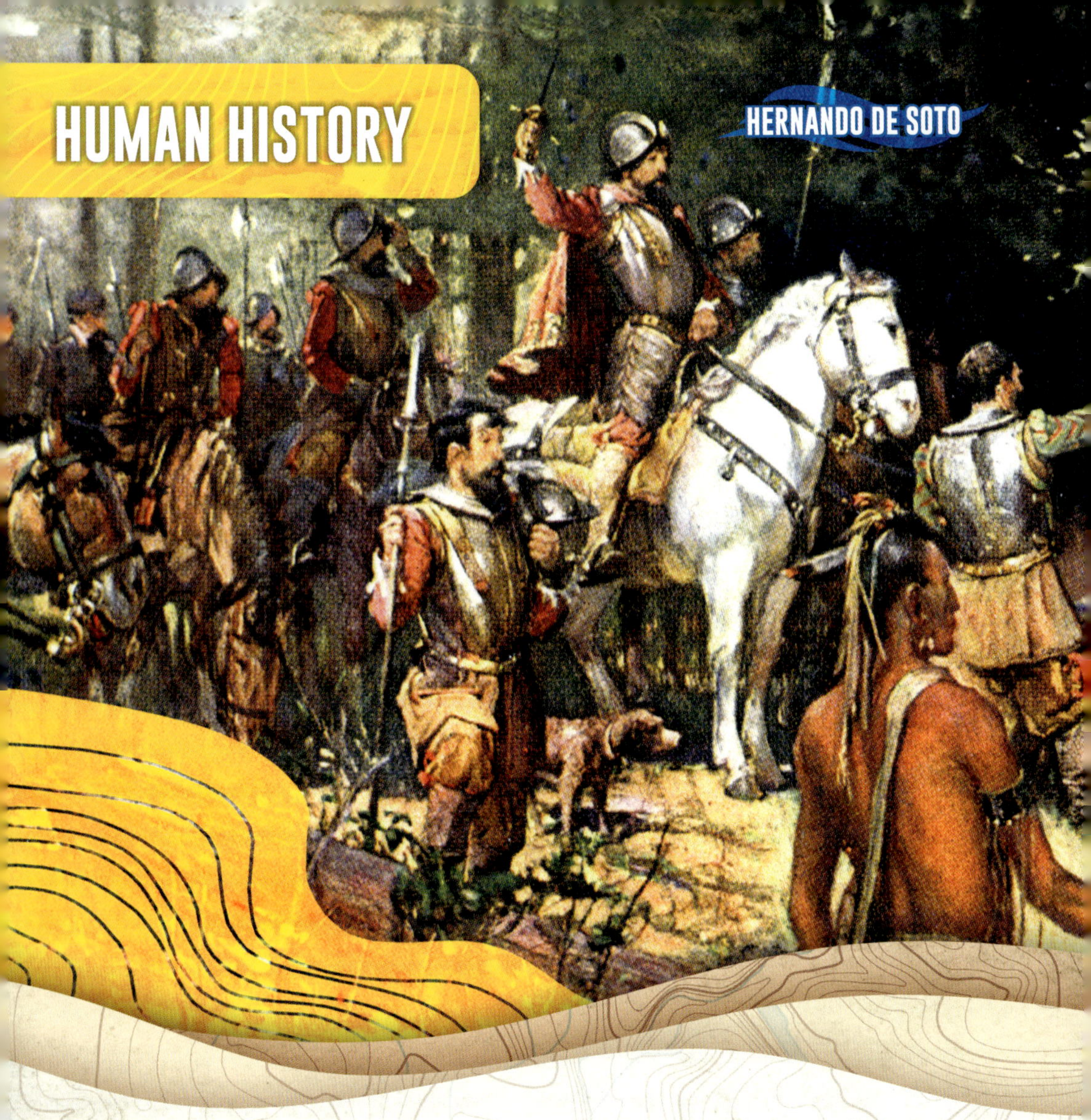
HERNANDO DE SOTO

People have hunted, fished, and gathered plants along the Mississippi River since about 10,000 BCE. Over time, they formed tribes. The river became important for travel and trade. The Ojibwe paddled birchbark canoes between northern villages. The Choctaw traded crops farmed on southern shores.

A HEALING RIVER

For centuries, Native American peoples have made medicines from river plants. The Ojibwe have used goldenrod to help with stomachaches and fevers.

CHOCTAW PEOPLE

In 1541, Spanish explorer Hernando de Soto became the first European to cross the Mississippi River. In 1673, French explorers Jacques Marquette and Louis Jolliet traveled from today's Lake Michigan to the Mississippi River. They followed the waterway south to present-day Arkansas. The explorers learned from Native American tribes that the river flowed to the Gulf of Mexico.

The Mississippi River became the western U.S. border in 1783. The country's boundaries expanded with the 1803 **Louisiana Purchase**. Some people built homes along the river. Soon small towns dotted the riverbanks.

CULTURAL CONNECTION

MARK TWAIN ON THE RIVER

BOOKS

The Adventures of Tom Sawyer and *The Adventures of Huckleberry Finn*

WHAT ARE THEY?

Classic books that give readers a sense of what life was like on the Mississippi River in the 1800s

WHO WROTE THEM?

Samuel Clemens, better known as Mark Twain

WHEN WERE THEY WRITTEN?

Late 1800s

MARK TWAIN

Traders loaded rafts and **keelboats** with goods to sell downstream. Return trips upstream were difficult. But the development of the **steamboat** allowed river traffic to go both ways. By the 1830s, more than 1,000 steamboats operated on the river. They carried passengers as well as cargo.

LOCK AND DAM

During the **Civil War**, the North won control of the Mississippi River. They used it to move supplies and invade cities in the South. The river also helped **enslaved** people escape north to freedom.

After the war, the U.S. Army Corps of Engineers (USACE) made parts of the river wider and deeper. It built a fleet of large boats to help move heavy cargo. In the 1930s, the government built a series of **locks** and dams in the north. Later, new channels were made through the delta. These features helped make the Mississippi a key shipping route.

MISSISSIPPI RIVER TIMELINE

10,000 BCE
Early people hunt and fish along the Mississippi River

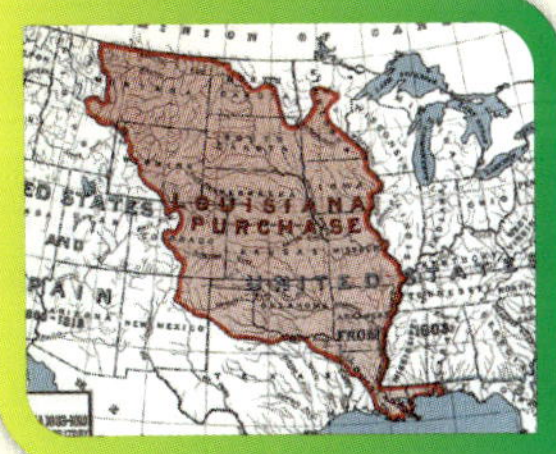

1541 CE
Spanish explorer Hernando de Soto crosses the Mississippi River

1803
The Louisiana Purchase gives the U.S. control of the whole Mississippi River Valley

1930s
The U.S. Army Corps of Engineers builds locks and dams to allow barges to operate in shallow parts of the river

2023
The government increases the area of the Middle Mississippi National Wildlife Refuge to protect and restore wildlife habitats

THE RIVER TODAY

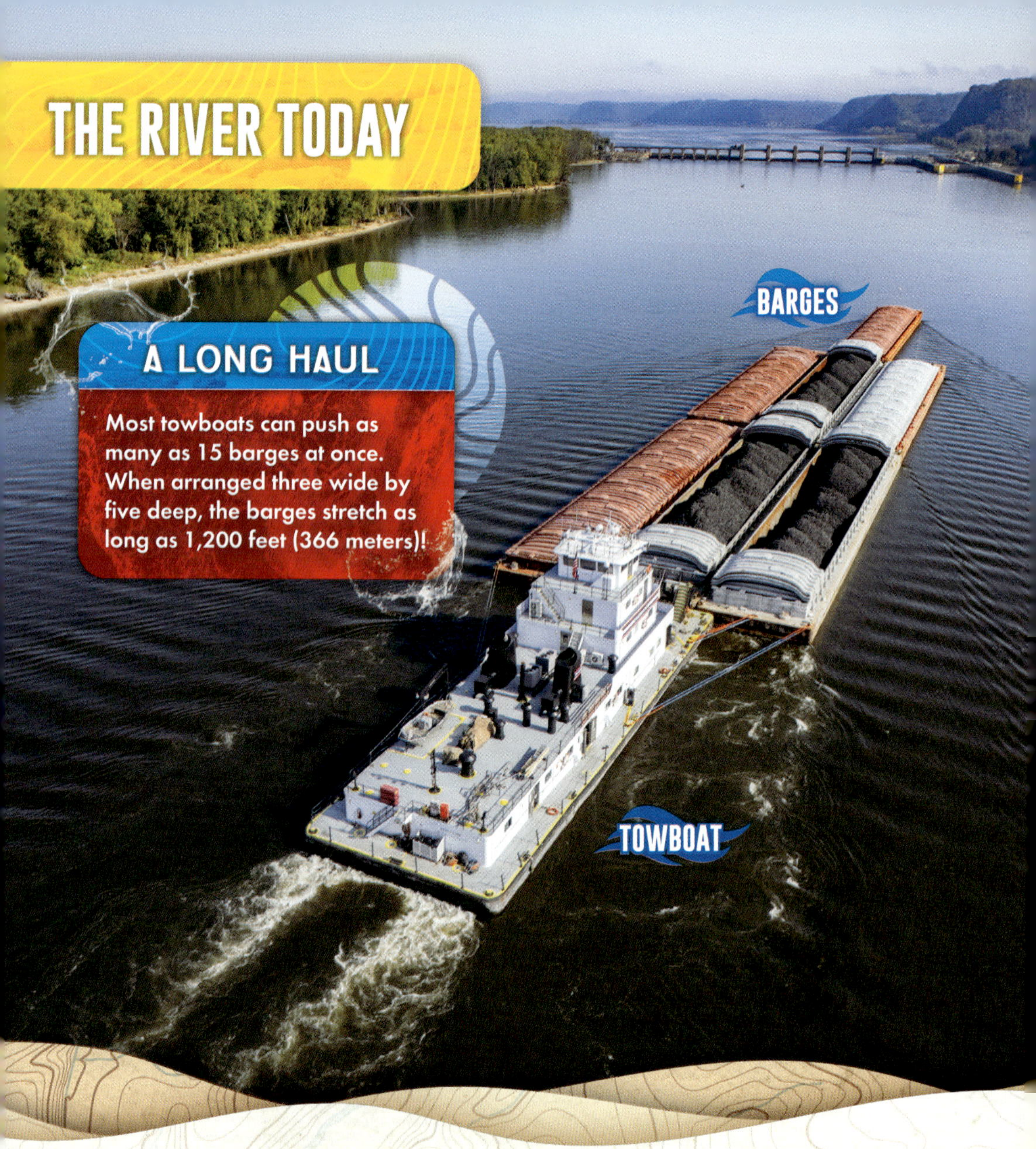

BARGES

TOWBOAT

A LONG HAUL

Most towboats can push as many as 15 barges at once. When arranged three wide by five deep, the barges stretch as long as 1,200 feet (366 meters)!

Today, the Mississippi River is one of the world's busiest waterways. **Towboats** push barges up and down the river. Barges are large, flat boats that carry heavy cargo. They often hold grain, coal, and other resources. From river ports, trucks and trains deliver cargo across the country.

The USACE maintains the river to keep boat traffic moving safely. They **dredge** the bottom to create a shipping channel deep enough for large vessels. The USACE also operates 29 locks and dams. This helps vessels travel safely between southern Minnesota and central Missouri.

RIVER PROJECT PROFILE

EADS BRIDGE

WHAT IS IT?

A bridge with three wide arches that connects St. Louis, Missouri, and East St. Louis, Illinois, and is the world's first steel bridge

PURPOSE

A major crossing over the Mississippi River for pedestrians, cars, and trains

COMPLETED

1874

GREAT RIVER ROAD

LEVEE

KAYAKER

In spring, melting snow and heavy rain can cause flooding. Engineers work to control how the Mississippi River overflows. Dams on the Missouri and Ohio tributaries limit the amount of water that can enter the Mississippi. **Levees** help contain the water. In some places, channels called floodways redirect water.

THE GREAT RIVER ROAD

The Great River Road is a protected National Scenic Byway. It is one of the longest roads of its kind in the U.S. It takes travelers through 10 states and hundreds of small river towns.

The Mississippi River is also a place for fun! Boaters zip across the water while canoers and kayakers paddle downstream. Hikers and bikers look for wildlife along riverside trails. Fishers cast their lines into the water. Cruise ships take passengers on scenic tours.

PROTECTING THE RIVER

Waste from homes, factories, and farms causes pollution. This harms people and wildlife along the Mississippi River. Groups that fight pollution pick up trash to keep the riverbanks clean. They support laws to stop people and businesses from polluting the river.

Climate change leads to more severe weather along the Mississippi River. Heavy rain can cause floods in nearby cities. Other areas experience long periods of dry weather, which lowers the river's water level. In the delta, this allows saltwater to flow farther inland. Plants and animals cannot survive. People lose access to safe drinking water.

LOW WATER LEVEL

POLLUTION

Swamps along the Mississippi River take in and hold water. They keep floodwaters away from populated places. But many of these areas have been cleared for buildings and roads. Dams that control flooding also keep water from plants and animals that need it. Many groups and government programs aim to restore these swamps.

The government manages national **wildlife refuges** on the Mississippi River. These large areas provide safe homes for plants and animals. Many refuges encourage people to visit and watch the river's wildlife. Visitors learn how important it is to protect this beautiful waterway!

GLOSSARY

channels—paths where water flows; channels often connect rivers to larger bodies of water.

Civil War—a war between the Northern (Union) and Southern (Confederate) states that lasted from 1861 to 1865

climate change—a human-caused change in Earth's weather due to warming temperatures

confluence—the place where two rivers meet

delta—a land area that forms where a river flows into a large body of water

dredge—to scoop out mud and weeds from the bottom of a lake, river, or other body of water

enslaved—considered property and forced to work for no pay

glaciers—massive sheets of ice that cover large areas of land

gulf—part of an ocean or sea that extends into land

keelboats—covered, flat-bottomed boats used to carry cargo

levees—mounds of earth built along the banks of a river to prevent flooding; levees can be natural or human-made.

locks—human-made waterways with gates at each end; locks change the water level to raise or lower boats.

Louisiana Purchase—a deal made between France and the United States; it gave the United States 828,000 square miles (2,144,510 square kilometers) of land west of the Mississippi River.

steamboat—a boat powered by a steam engine; steam engines are engines that generate power with steam.

towboats—boats with square fronts for pushing barges down a river

tributaries—rivers and streams that flow into a larger stream, river, or lake

wildlife refuges—areas set aside to protect plants, animals, land, and water

TO LEARN MORE

AT THE LIBRARY

Agnone, Julie Vosburgh. *Amazing Rivers: 100+ Waterways that Will Boggle Your Mind.* Greenbelt, Md.: What on Earth Books, 2021.

Mehnert, Volker. *Great Rivers of the World.* New York, N.Y.: Prestel Publishing, 2021.

Scott, David. *The Mississippi and Other U.S. Waterways.* Huntington Beach, Calif.: Teacher Created Materials, 2023.

ON THE WEB

FACTSURFER

Factsurfer.com gives you a safe, fun way to find more information.

1. Go to www.factsurfer.com.
2. Enter "Mississippi River" into the search box and click 🔍.
3. Select your book cover to see a list of related content.

INDEX

The images in this book are reproduced through the courtesy of: DutcherAerials, front cover; Camptoloma, p. 3; John Warburton-Lee Photography/ Alamy, p. 4; John_Brueske, pp. 4-5; Photo Image, p. 6; marekuliasz, p. 8 (top and bottom); Lena Platonova, p. 9; David S Swierczek, p. 10; Jaimie Tuchman, p. 11 (top); Hemis/ Alamy, p. 11 (bottom); Geoffrey Kuchera, p. 12 (bobcat); imageBROKER.com, p. 12 (eastern gray squirrel); Tom Reichner, p. 12 (green frog); Rostislav Stefanek, p. 12 (largemouth bass); Robert Adami, p. 12 (mallard ducks); Vladimir Turkenich, p. 13; photo.malte, p. 14 (top); Pierre Jean Durieu, p. 14 (bottom); Lowell Monke, p. 15; ClassicStock/ Alamy, pp. 16-17; MPI/ Stringer/ Getty Images, p. 17; World History Archive/ Alamy, p. 18; Archive Pics/ Alamy, p. 19; John Brueske, p. 20; John Sartain/ Wikipedia, p. 21 (top); Hum Historical/ Alamy, p. 21 (middle); Aaron J Hill, p. 21 (bottom); John Touscany, p. 22; dvande, p. 23 (top); JL Jahn, p. 23 (bottom); Justin Wilkens, p. 24 (left); Dr. Victor Wong, p. 24 (right); Jeffrey K Collins, pp. 24-25; Steve Heap, p. 26; Art Wager, p. 27; 7Michael, pp. 28-29; Sandra Burm, p. 29; Jody Ann, p. 31.